Work-Life Fusion

A Guide to Freedom and Autonomy at Work

I0467689

Donna L. Haeger

Eilysh Haeger

To people of all ages as we navigate a changing world and strive to remain connected in the ways that matter.

Contents

Foreword

This book has two authors!

I've been researching elements of work-life fusion since the year 2011. After years of research, I enlisted the help of my daughter, Eilysh, to turn what I've discovered into a format that is accessible to all.

Our intent is to provide an insightful introduction to the phenomenon of work-life fusion that is happening all around us. As technology becomes increasingly integrated into our lives, the way we approach work and life is changing.

We outline key characteristics of how different generational groups leverage technology in the workplace. Because there are so many differences between generations, we offer a shared understanding in an effort to blend human systems.

Blending human systems is meant to help people understand each other so they can experience successful interactions at work. We all do things differently and understanding each other goes a long way toward developing harmony between people both at work and in our daily lives.

In addition, we offer insights to employers and managers that can help with policies related to technology use at work. There is a lot of research proving that people who have positive interactions at work are happier and more productive. People who feel free and autonomous at work are also more likely to stay in their jobs longer.

We consider a workplace hosting multiple generations to be ripe for cultivating generational sensitivity and awareness.

Our world is a diverse one. As such, we hope this book helps people better understand how to embrace generational differences.

Introduction

In the year 2015, Millennials surpassed Gen Xers as the largest generation in the U.S. workforce.[1] As technology catapults us into the future, the nature and approach to work is changing rapidly.

The newest generation to the workforce grew up with access to technology such as computers, cell phones, and the Internet. With access to these tools, the way they manage both their work and their lives is far different from the generations preceding them.

Millennials are fully adapted to the new paradigm. But what paradigm is that?

How does a twenty-year-old approach the workplace compared to a fifty-year old?

The answer may be more complex than you think.

What once was a simple way of managing work and life has evolved into a myriad of different approaches, all influenced by technology. Like the Industrial Revolution of the past, the advent of the digital age has led to a shift in the way people of different generations manage their work and personal lives.

Each generation brings not only their talents and skills to the work environment, but also their own expectations. These differences often result in conflict and unnecessary frustration.

Consider the manager that can't understand a worker's attachment to her smartphone. Or the young leader that can't get his senior employees to learn a new software at the drop of a hat.

These collisions are part of a fundamental difference in perception and exposure when it comes to technology and work-life management.

The workplace is a dynamic thing no matter what type of lifestyle you live or organization you work for. To navigate this ever-changing environment, understanding others is crucial.

Managers who can understand differences that exist within their team, are better equipped to foster relationships, and lead successfully.

Likewise, employers who can create a comfortable and productive environment for their employees will be more likely to retain talent.

Dependence on technology has increased exponentially over the past decade to the point that it has become omnipresent. Due to this influx of technology, the ways in which we perform our jobs is shifting.

Millennials are the first generation in which this change is apparent. For them, work and personal life do not exist separately, but concurrently, in a fused state in which each overlaps the other seamlessly.

Based on several research studies I conducted both as a doctoral student and a faculty member, this book explores the current shift in the workplace—a shift I call work-life fusion.

As people utilize new technology in their jobs, organizational policies continue to develop around what is or isn't appropriate in the workplace. Policies which, if restrictive, can greatly affect an employee's job satisfaction. These policies affect generational groups differently and impact how people understand each other at work. To foster productivity and teamwork, we must strive to have a shared understanding of how we each approach work and life.

Therein lies the greatest benefits in understanding work-life fusion.

Happy workers stay in their jobs. This decreases turnover and reduces expenses related to recruitment. Companies and business owners that can accommodate an environment where work-life fusion has become the norm will be able to retain more employees and therefore increase profits.

In turn, employees that can understand what they need in their work environment, will have more direct control over their job satisfaction and be able to improve their satisfaction with life.

Now is the time to understand how our work environments are changing. Everyone has a different perspective and experience of technology and it carries over into the workplace.

When you can better understand your coworkers, you can work together more effectively.

When you understand your own individual needs at work, you will be better equipped to find a job in a work culture that suits you.

Change is upon us and no matter your generation, we are all adapting. For more than a century, we've managed to keep our work separate from both our personal life and our personal identity, but that time has passed.

Work and life have collided.

The age of work-life fusion is upon us.

Part I

Past and Present

1

The Evolution of Work and Life

Work-life fusion is the newest form of work-life management.

The history of managing work and life goes back over a century to the dawn of the Industrial Revolution. Though remembered as a time of poor pay, long hours, and bad working conditions, the Industrial Revolution signaled a critical moment in the lives of workers. It was during this era that the realms of work and life first became segmented.

No longer did work consist of farming the family lands and shipping off produce as it did in the largely agricultural society of the past. People flocked to cities where work became something that was situated outside the home. People woke up in the morning and went to the factory, or the textile mill, or the coal mine. While they were there, they worked and did little else.

Only after a long day of putting in hours to obtain a living wage did workers depart for home and resume their personal lives. The next day, they would do it all over again.

It wasn't until the weekend that one could spend the day with family and friends, indulge in hobbies, and enjoy the fruits of his labor.

This strict divide between work and life was a direct result of industrialization. The old model of men going to work and women running the household was completely upended.

As women, both single and married, entered the workforce, a new concern was work-life management and how a working person could better juggle and reconcile her work and personal life.

In the early years of the Industrial Revolution, most studies in the workplace focused on maximizing production. It was widely believed that if you manufactured it, people would buy it. As a result, the goal became to produce as much as possible.

This led to the era of time-motion studies which investigated how long it took a person to complete certain tasks to create a product. Refinements would be made to the assembly line, including where machines were placed on the floor, so people could walk to them more quickly. The idea was that saving just seconds to create one item would equate to more products made in the same amount of time.

This was considered an economy of scale since you could essentially produce more products in the day without paying more workers, paying overtime, or running the machines longer. No additional money was spent, but more was produced which led to higher revenue and profit.

In the 1920's Elton Mayo and Fritz Roethlisberger began what became known as the Hawthorne studies, at a plant of the Western Electric Company. The original goal was to see if people in the plant were more productive at different levels of lighting. They measured output and talked with workers.

After taking numerous measurements, they discovered that at all levels of lighting, productivity had increased. Even after they returned to the usual level of lighting, for some reason, people were producing more. They discovered that as investigators walked around and talked with workers, the perception was that they were cared for and their opinions were valued. This made them happier in their jobs and made them want to work harder.

Thus, the "human factors" movement was born. Instead of solely focusing on people and machines as producers, studies began to emphasize the socio-psychological aspects of human behavior in organizations.

After nearly a century of such studies, we now know that quality of work life is critical to things like job satisfaction, work-life satisfaction, and a sense of well-being with life in general. Most importantly, the idea of autonomy and freedom at work has surfaced as a strong influencer of these outcomes.

People like to feel trusted and free at work. They like their employers to allow them the latitude to get their jobs done without hovering and they desire the freedom to control where, when, and how they do their jobs.[2]

Researchers call this psychological job control; otherwise known as the amount of freedom and autonomy you perceive you have in your job.

Employers have kept abreast of workplace studies that relate to employee happiness and satisfaction and many have implemented polices to promote employee wellbeing in an effort to maximize productivity and reduce turnover.

As technology becomes more and more a part of our daily lives, certain tools and their availability at work has a larger impact on a person's perceived autonomy at work. People, and especially companies, are interested in the quality of a person's work life and how this influences the way one feels about his job. Research into the predicament of how best to balance work and life has revealed interesting conclusions about employee satisfaction.

In 2005, a research study examined the new trend of telecommuting and how it affected the amount of autonomy workers perceived they had in their job.[2] They found that the more control people felt they had over where, when, and how they worked, the lower their depression, work and family life conflict, and turnover intention.

Telecommuting marked a significant change in the way people manage their personal and professional lives. Since the advent of the Internet and the digital age, we've been hurtling toward a new way of living and working. As technology such as email, texting, and social media continues to influence us in all areas of life, the separation is disappearing.

Work and life have folded in on each other and are merging in new and unexpected ways. This new pattern is apparent in the way it manifests across generations.

Today, the most prominent age groups in the workforce are the Baby Boomer, Gen X, and Millennial generations. Named for the birthrate spike that occurred after the Second World War, the Baby Boomers were born between the years 1946 and 1964. The latchkey generation, or Gen X, is broadly defined as those born between 1965 and the late 1970's. Lastly, the Millennials are identified as the generation born between 1980 and the early 2000's, or those who came of age during the new millennium.

Each group has unique life experiences as well as different levels of technology immersion that have shaped how they think, perceive, and approach the world.

On a continuum, we can see that Boomers have had the least exposure to digital tools in their formative years and have learned to leverage digital technology as it became available. At the other end of the spectrum, Millennials were born into the digital age and thus have little to no experience of life without digital technology.

As technology continues to advance, we are moving away from a balancing act of work and life and are instead entering the era of the fused work environment. Millennials are part of an unprecedented phenomenon in which work and life are managed as a whole, integrated to the point that they are virtually inseparable.

Seventy-five million Millennials are already fused, but they alone do not drive the need for a technological workplace. Both similarities and differences exist in how all three generations manage work and life.

When all must share the workplace, understanding these differences is vital, especially when access to technology has the power to influence a worker's sense of freedom and autonomy. With job satisfaction on the line, no business can afford to ignore the needs of the increasingly diverse workforce.

In the beginning, the areas of work and life became separated due to industrialization. After decades of studying people at work, we now know that the quality of work life, particularly the amount of freedom and autonomy at work, is essential in keeping people satisfied with their jobs.

The problem is that there isn't a one-size-fits-all solution. With three different generations making up the majority of the workforce and technology constantly changing the environment of the workplace, understanding others is of paramount importance.

What does work-life fusion have to do with this?

It could be the key to understanding ourselves in relation to technology.

2

What is Work-Life Fusion?

Work-life fusion is the newest form of work-life management. It is perfectly tailored for a technological age and fully customizable based on the needs of digital workers.

The notion of work and life as two parts of a whole has been studied and written about since the 1970's. This goal and elusive formula for equilibrium have been at the forefront of personal and managerial agendas for years.

The topic can be traced back to the Industrial Revolution within a framework where work and life existed as two distinct domains and the challenge was to manage them separately.

Work	Home

Organizations have spent countless hours and dollars in an effort to understand the needs of employees in order to develop successful policies and programs to help with this issue.

Today, we have seen technology infused into the workplace and we have seen generations of people immersed in technology from birth. This influx of technology is shifting how people manage both their work and their life, drastically changing the two-dimensional approach to balancing our lives. This immersion in technology now allows us to manage our work and personal lives together and at the same time.

This is the definition of work–life fusion; the simultaneous management of work and life demands.

Work-life fusion is a paradigm shift, or a change in basic assumptions, when it comes to work and life management.

Fusion has become our new normal, but the degree to which you are immersed in technology changes the degree to which you are currently fused. Depending on your age and upbringing, there can be stark contrasts.

With our work environment becoming more complex and diverse, creative methods and approaches such as flexible work hours, maternity/paternity leave, and working at home have emerged. This has not been a subtle shift as advancements in technology have swept like a tsunami into all areas of our lives.

Essentially, work and life have fused through technology and this has re-landscaped everything, including the workplace. People are taking work and life systems and using technology as the means to merge them into a single, fused system which is stronger and more sustainable.

In this way, you can think of work-life fusion as work-life management on steroids, with technology acting as the enhancement.

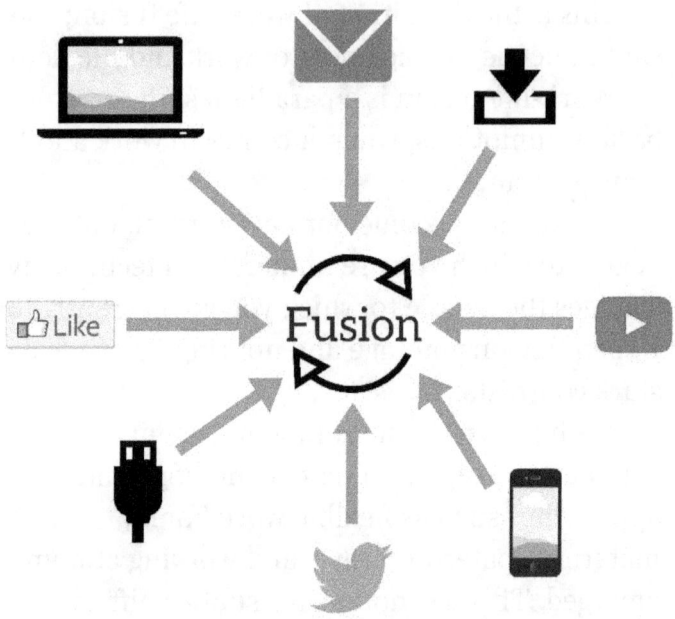

Depending on your age, work-life fusion may be so much a part of you that you aren't even aware that there's a different way of approaching the world. There is a clear indication that the fused approach toward work and life management increases as people become younger. The first truly fused generation are the Millennials, the generation immersed in technology since birth.

This new paradigm for work and life is in sharp contrast to the way older workers understand and experience it. In the past, people experienced pressures to balance work commitments and personal commitments separately. If you had a day job, you managed personal activities when the workday was done.

Young workers are not concerned with work and life as separate entities and prefer to give up the physical world for a virtual one where they manage these aspects of their lives concurrently.

While older workers comfortably balance the worlds of work and life separately and in specific time periods,[3] new workers strike this balance virtually using technology. The physical and virtual worlds happen simultaneously for young workers. They manage their worlds in a nonlinear and 24/7 fashion, periodically checking in to one or the other.

This is not to say that older workers do not work in a fused manner, they certainly do, but at a different level. Boomers still have the unique ability to separate work and life while others may not be conscious of such a separation.

While work/life balance may not be dead, fusion is quickly becoming our new normal. The younger you are, the more technological immersion you have experienced at a young age, therefore the more fused your approach to work and life.

Technology has shifted the way we view work and life, changing the common goal of striking a balance between our work and personal responsibilities. With the workplace changing more rapidly than ever before, the question becomes, are our work and personal lives still truly separate?

We can only answer this by starting at the beginning, at the point before the concept of work-life fusion existed.

Part II

The Study

3

The Generation Gap: Intriguing Differences Between Boomers and Millennials in the Workplace

It all began with the Baby Boomers and the Millennials, two very different generations that are also surprisingly similar. Their similarities, however, are a discussion for a later chapter. This is the story of their most intriguing difference, the discovery that birthed the term "work-life fusion".

Technically, it all began with a single finding.

In 2010, I was a newly minted Ph.D. student about to embark on my first journey of research. My main interest lay in studying leadership and how people of different generations lead and follow in the workplace.

At the time, my goal was to dig deeper into human systems such as the relationship between leaders and subordinates. I was passionate about better understanding groups of people that are different and whether or not age influences how one leads in the workplace.

I designed a study[4] that involved interviewing both Millennial leaders and people at least twenty years older who reported to Millennial leaders. The focus of the study was leadership approach and how it compared to employee expectations of the leader.

It wasn't long before a notable pattern began to surface. In my conversations with Millennial leaders and employees who belonged to the Baby Boomer generation, I discovered opposing perspectives of work and how it should be managed with one's personal life.

The words that one group used to describe work and life conflicted with the way the other explained their management of these same areas.

For instance, Boomers still talked about work/life balance and how it related to their sense of job and life satisfaction. Millennials, on the other hand, described managing work and life at the same time through technology.

One important discovery was that Boomers seemed to be experiencing significant stress when reporting to a younger leader. As is their norm, they felt the need to turn off work and return to their lives at the end of each work day. They couldn't fathom why their Millennial leader seemed oblivious to this lifestyle when it had been customary for as long as they could remember.

For example, Millennial leaders were surprised if emails were not answered over the weekend. Alternatively, Boomer direct reports felt that when Millennial leaders checked their phone during a meeting, it meant a lack of interest in the work.

It turned out that Millennials, as leaders, were not accommodating these differences in their workers because they were not aware such a need existed. They did not seem to separate work and life the way Boomers did.

That was all the invitation I needed to dive head first into further research.

What might be going on with technology use?

I had to find the underlying cause of this startling difference and more closely examine how people were managing work and life through technology.

In April of 2011, I set out to study how people leveraged technology at work. I sensed there was something new happening inside this notion of work/life balance.

In a survey, I asked 500 people various questions about the need for technological tools and virtual contact with others, both at work and in their personal lives. In addition, I inquired about their use of email, social media, webcam, and phone technologies.

I initially called this study[5] the New Work/Life Balance.

Yet when I divided the results between different generations, it became clear that this was not a new form of work/life balance at all.

Boomers could still compartmentalize work and life. However, technology-immersed Millennials had no notion of work and life having any sort of boundary. With technology as their aid, Millennials had completely fused the management of their work and life experiences.

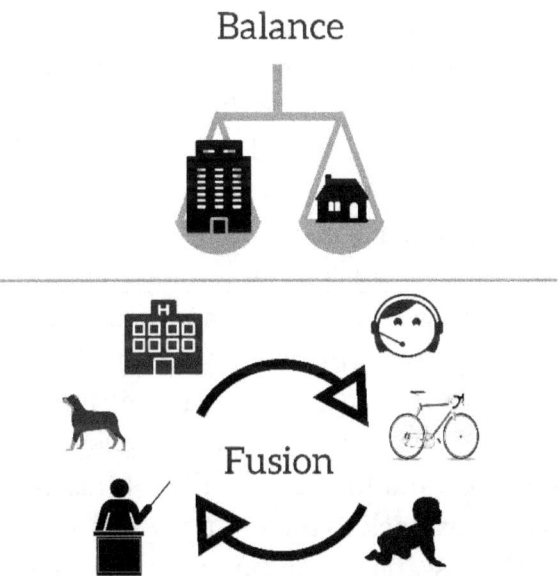

In addition, all ages agreed that face-to-face interaction was no longer critical and that a virtual environment was the new normal. The only exception was the Millennials, who consider a virtual environment to be *the* normal, since they do not recognize any alternative.

The study also asked people if there was a need to concurrently tend to work and life issues during the day. Not surprisingly, both Gen Xers and Millennials felt this was critical to their sense of freedom at work.

I checked all the digital tools as they related to job satisfaction and work-life satisfaction.

What I found was that Boomers, while using some tech at work, did not report feeling any loss of freedom in the absence of it.

Gen Xers and Millennials both agreed that they felt freer and more successful in balancing work and life issues when these tools were available. However, they diverged in that this freedom, or lack thereof, clearly impacted Millennial job satisfaction while Gen Xers could remain content in their jobs without it.

For Millennials, the absence of an environment supporting work-life fusion was considered an affront to their freedom and they were having none of it. The findings of this study gave birth to the topic of my dissertation and further, the title of this book.

Thinking back to the interviews in my first study, a lot of the dissatisfaction Boomers were having with Millennial leaders centered around a lack of understanding regarding how differently each generation approaches work and life.

As one Boomer states, "My work life is work and my home life is my home life. It's always been that way. With a younger manager, on the other hand, everything is open, everything is fair game. The younger manager feels, 'My life is my work, my work is my life'. And they don't seem to have a problem mixing the two or getting too messy."

While many Boomers today leverage technology for work and life management, they are still hard-wired to compartmentalize and do not become stressed when doing so. In fact, this ability may lead to higher rates of job and life satisfaction.

In direct contrast to this, Millennials in an environment where the fused management approach is not supported, report being stressed and unhappy at work. If they cannot manage their work and personal lives simultaneously, they feel stifled at best and at worst, will quit their jobs.

I knew this phenomenon had strong implications for organizational success and the way people interact at work.

Blending people with technology already has its own set of implications further complicated by adding the dimension of age. Not only is it important to understand different perspectives when it comes to managing work and life, but organizations must consider these differences if they are striving to reduce turnover and raise the bottom line.

Since a work environment can directly impact employee satisfaction and well-being, an organization can't afford to ignore the needs of different workers when it comes to rules and policies regarding technology use in the workplace.

Through research, I was able to uncover a new approach to work-life management, primarily utilized by Millennials. My first study focused on leadership among different generations, but revealed a key disconnect between Millennial leaders and their Baby Boomer employees. Next, I discovered that technology was the main cause of this disconnect and that's why Baby Boomers and Millennials were approaching work differently.

In my most recent study, I examined the concept of what I call "work-life fusion" by honing in on which technological tools each generation uses to manage their work and personal lives. This is critical in understanding how members of different generations feel about technology and how this influences their sense of freedom and autonomy at work.

Freedom and autonomy are the ultimate endgame when it comes to having happy employees. This is because freedom and autonomy affect everything.

Today, we don't want independence and flexibility in our job just because it will make us satisfied with our work. We want the ability to control where, when, and how we do our job because it will make managing the other half of our life—the half full of friends, family, and personal responsibilities—easier.

4

Freedom and Autonomy: Why Independence Matters at Work

The term *work-life satisfaction* is defined as how happy you are with the way you divide your time between work responsibilities and personal responsibilities. Essentially what it measures is a person's contentment with how they distribute their time between work and life commitments.

When I designed my final study[6] in 2016—the one I hoped would reveal further insight into the phenomenon of work-life fusion—I decided to find out which tools people used to manage work and which they used to manage personal life. As I did this, I gauged the impact these tools had on an employee's sense of freedom and autonomy.

Based on the interviews I conducted as well as casual conversations I'd had with people, I chose to focus specifically on email, texting and social media. I asked people how these tools, and the virtual environment at work, made them feel about their ability to get work done. I also asked how this influenced the way they felt about their jobs, their work-life satisfaction, and their satisfaction with life in general.

Specifically, what I was looking for was whether the availability of technology at work made people feel like they had the freedom and autonomy to get their jobs done. When it comes to managing work and life, autonomy is the personal freedom someone has to control where, when, and how she does her job. This is important because a person's perceived autonomy in her job can affect both her job and work-life satisfaction. Since turnover is the single largest expenditure for most businesses, keeping people happy and in their jobs can make a business much more profitable.

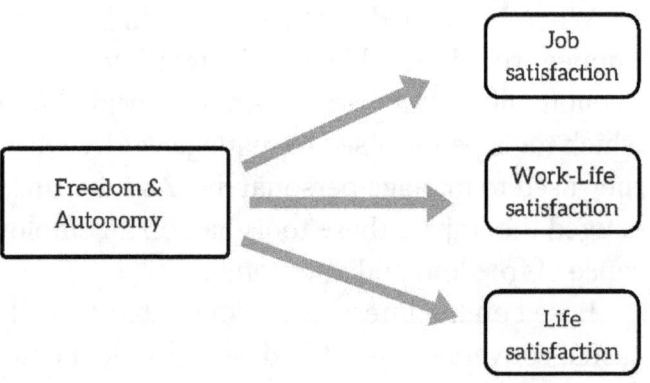

What I found is that some age groups do not lose their sense of freedom and autonomy in the absence of technology, while others feel it in a significant way.

Personally, I am in the unique position of being neither a Baby Boomer nor a Millennial. As a member of Generation X, I have witnessed firsthand how people both older and younger than me approach work.

Like many, I've experienced the influx of technology that characterizes the digital age. From computers to cell phones to tablets, I've adapted to new technology at a pace that my ancestors could never have imagined.

I've seen my Baby Boomer mother transform from using a typewriter in her daily job to operating a home office complete with laptop, cell phone, and iPad. I've also experienced how my children, immersed in technology since birth, have been the catalyst for my own introduction to social media apps like Snapchat and Instagram.

With the influence of technology nearly inescapable, each generation manifests the way they live and work differently. Each group brings their own technological expectations and experiences to the workplace, whether they are conscious of it or not.

The main difference between Baby Boomers and Millennials is not just the kind of technology they are using at work, but what they are using this technology for. Using email to get work done is one thing, but checking personal email, texting friends, and checking Facebook during your work day is another.

With these technologies at our disposal, the possibilities for managing work and life are endless. How we spend our time tending to work and life responsibilities greatly depends on when we were born and what kind of expectations we have about our workplace.

The work-life fusion study examined how tools like email, texting, and social media affect a person's sense of freedom and autonomy at work. At the same time, it examined how different generations used these technologies to manage their work versus their personal lives.

The way each generation approaches technology may surprise you or it may be very familiar.

Society's movement toward work-life fusion is a shift that some take for granted, but technological freedom at work can have a lasting impact, influencing how happy and free employees perceive themselves to be. Depending on a person's age, happiness can be tied mildly or catastrophically to technology use in the workplace.

Part III

Baby Boomers

5

Technology Use For Work: Staying Happy on the Job

The technology Baby Boomers prefer for work is the result of years of technological innovation.

Prior to widespread email usage, ink and paper ruled the day. For thousands of years, our ancestors scribbled, scratched, and scrawled with a collection of pigments and dyes known as ink.

Whether it was to record history, communicate publicly, or send correspondence to loved ones far away, writing with ink was the primary means of sending messages when you couldn't be face to face.

Today, some say letter-writing is a lost art. Although the physical act of putting pen to paper hasn't lost its value, nowadays it has a fierce competitor.

Since the advent of the printing press in the 1400's, we've been rushing headlong into an era of mass communication. Email is one technology that plays a large role in this age of information.

Let me ask you something.

When did you last check your email?

I'm willing to bet it was within the past few hours. Maybe the past few minutes.

With email at our fingertips, communication with colleagues, friends, and family is mere seconds away.

But it wasn't always this way.

If you think about the technology we use for communication today, it all came about because of email.

Email was invented in the 1960's and became commonplace in many organizations by the 1970's. Early messaging systems were closed systems mainly used for inter-organizational communication. In the beginning, it was more like instant messaging where people could only send messages if they were both logged in at the same time.

By the 1980's, the Advanced Research Projects Agency Network (ARPANET), and a protocol called TCP/IP jointly allowed for the system we call the Internet to be developed.[7] With the explosion of the Internet, network-based email systems flourished— first in the workplace and then later as a personal tool.

Today, the Internet allows for both stored email and real time communication to happen between people anywhere. There are at least 2.5 billion email users worldwide, millions of which access email from a mobile device on a daily basis.[8] This explosive use of email has greatly transformed businesses and organizations by becoming the primary means for both internal and external communications.

When you think about it, most technology became commonplace at work before it ever became a household utility. This was due to the cost and size of the machines involved. After all, the first computers took up an entire room and could cost thousands, if not millions, of dollars.

Today, technology has become pervasive in both work and personal life, spurring the new paradigm of work-life fusion. New technology is something we can count on, especially in the workplace.

For decades, we've seen technology streamline processes and transform the way we work and communicate. For example, when my mother first entered the workplace, it looked very different than it does today. In her early work as a secretary, she learned to take dictation and how to write things shorthand. Of course, if something needed to be printed fast, she used a typewriter. This was the norm for decades before the invention of the computer.

It wasn't until my mother went to college in her late 30's that she first encountered what we consider modern technology. By the time she got her law degree, she knew how to use a computer.

Throughout her career as a lawyer, my mother has had to learn a variety of new technologies, her workplace transforming greatly since her typewriter days. A member of the Baby Boomer generation, she has embraced the challenge of learning new things. She's gone from using a corded, land-line telephone to mastering the smartphone and she's even delved into new territory like posting on Instagram and sending Snapchats to me and her grandchildren.

Digital tools and technology do not scare my mother, but they are certainly not something she was exposed to early in life. Unlike my children, who could operate a computer by age three, my mother has had to learn along the way how to use and apply new technology. Email, for instance, is a tool that has made communication in my mother's work easier and more efficient.

In my work-life fusion study, I found that she is not an unusual case.

According to the research, Baby Boomers find email a useful tool for getting work done and having access to it contributes to their job satisfaction. When Boomers can use email in their jobs to communicate and complete work assignments, they are happier with their jobs.

When asked how they would feel if they weren't allowed to use email to get work done, Boomers reported that it would be mildly inconvenient, but they would not feel stressed or confined.

What this means is that email is an important tool for a Boomer's job satisfaction. Because they've experienced a time before email existed, however, they aren't dependent on it to get their job done. For a Boomer, email in the workplace is a modern luxury and convenience.

If my mother couldn't use email to get work done, she might be less happy with her job. However, she would probably revert to using her phone to contact clients and be able to accomplish her tasks, regardless.

But what if a Boomer couldn't text? Or use social media to do their work? Would it matter?

The answer would depend upon the nature of the job, of course, and as a public defender, my mother doesn't necessarily use social media in her daily work. As a Boomer, however, she has a certain relationship with technology that is different from generations born after her.

Similar to email, texting and instant messaging (IM) are technologies that entered the workplace in the midst of my mother's career.

SMS (short message service) was first used in 1992 when British engineer Neil Papworth sent a single text from his computer across town to his friend's Orbitel 901 mobile phone.[9] His friend couldn't reply because his phone had no way of inputting text.

Texting is great for communicating brief messages such as informing a friend you'll be late or reminding a colleague about a meeting. Allowing for direct communication without having to be face to face, texting has helped transform the way we live and work.

Similarly, instant messaging has helped to facilitate work transactions. Modern types of instant messaging services first took off in the mid 1990's. You might remember PowWow or AOL Instant Messenger, two of the very first Internet chat programs.

Although texting and IM were mainly used for social and personal purposes, today they are used in business, government, and other organizations for communication between coworkers. Like email, sending texts and instant messages has become an accepted part of our culture.

When asked how they used IM and texting at work and whether this affected their sense of autonomy, my study found that Baby Boomers feel a loss of autonomy at work when they cannot text or IM to get their jobs done. This means that Boomers are now utilizing IM and texting to communicate within their organization in order to complete their work. In fact, they feel a greater loss without this tool than they do if email is not available!

So, it's important to know that having access to these tools in order to perform their job duties, gives Boomers a greater sense of freedom and autonomy at work. Without access to messaging services such as Skype Instant Messenger or Google Hangouts, Boomers would likely feel a lack of personal freedom to control where, when, and how they do their jobs. Employers need to be aware of this.

Social media falls into the same category as email for Baby Boomers. They also experience a level of job satisfaction when they have access to social media for work, but this does not affect how much freedom they perceive they have in their jobs.

Using social media for work can make a Boomer, like my mother, happier and more content with her job, but without access to social networking sites, she would still consider herself to have the freedom and independence to decide how to get her work done. In other words, she could live without it.

At work, Boomers experience an increased sense of freedom and autonomy if they can use texting and IM to get the job done. These technologies impact their satisfaction with their job as well as their satisfaction with the way they manage their work and personal responsibilities. Having access to these tools can even make them happier with their lives.

For Boomers, tools of convenience include email and social media. While not required, Baby Boomers do benefit from access to these tools at work and are more satisfied with their jobs because of them.

6

Technology Use For Personal Life: Connected While at Work

Using technology to stay connected with friends and family while at work is a fairly new phenomenon.

When my mother first entered the workforce, staying connected to your personal life during the work day was unheard of unless you were in special circumstances such as working as an employee in your family's business.

Picture this:

It's the year 1968.

The concept of a "9 to 5" job is in full swing.

As soon as you enter your employer's building, you report to your desk and settle in to start on your work tasks for the day. You're a young Baby Boomer working your way up the corporate ladder and you are dedicated to your career.

Your thoughts are no longer on your personal life, you already shut that off when you walked through the door. You're here to work, to earn a living, to help your colleagues, the business, and therefore help yourself. You've got a stable, dependable income and the only way to maintain that is to continue to perform, to arrive at work each day ready to do your job.

You might have the occasional thought about your spouse or kids or wonder what you'll be eating for dinner, but it doesn't matter right now. You'll figure that out later, after work hours or when you break for lunch—only once you've clocked out of the office.

Unless it's an emergency, it doesn't even occur to you to contact your loved ones. If you really needed to, there's the office phone. You could potentially ask to use it on your break.

Even though it's frowned upon, it's possible to call a family member while at work. Of course, your company would have to pay for the call and you are the average Baby Boomer, committed to your work. Calling home during work hours is for extenuating circumstances only.

In the evening, you leave for home, your work for the day complete. You exit the premises and resume your other life—the life outside your company, your coworkers, your career.

This is how it used to be...before technology like email and cell phones burst onto the scene and the traditional paradigm shattered.

According to the Radicati Group, an office worker today sends and receives an average of 120 emails per day.[8]

When I researched Boomers' relationship with email I found that they are no longer completely separating their work from their personal lives. Due to the influence of technology, Boomers are slowly adapting to work-life fusion and utilizing email at work to stay in touch with family and friends.

In fact, Boomers place a strong emphasis on the need for this connection to personal life. If they cannot use email for this purpose, they feel a loss of freedom and autonomy in their job. This contrasts with how they feel about using email for work. They like it, but can live without it.

This means that if an employer were to forbid a Boomer from using email for personal purposes during work hours, his sense of personal freedom to control where, when, and how he does his job is likely to suffer. This has major implications for employers seeking to reduce turnover by keeping workers happy.

On a similar note, the freedom to text friends and family while at work also affects Baby Boomers in their jobs. Results show that Boomers need to be able to text at work for personal life management.

When asked how they used texting at work and whether this impacted their sense of autonomy, Boomers were in strong agreement that the ability to text in order to remain connected to their personal lives makes them more satisfied with their job and creates a greater sense of satisfaction with life in general. Not only this, but the freedom to text for personal matters while at work, makes them happier with the way they divide their time between their job and personal life.

In other words, the freedom and autonomy to text for personal life, even during the work day, has become an important new requirement for Baby Boomers in the workplace. Where once there was no such need to contact family or friends while at work, now expectations have shifted with the influx of technology.

Boomers view emailing and texting for their personal lives favorably. This is certainly a culture shift for Boomers at work. When it comes to social media, however, things get interesting.

Kids in this day in age don't think twice about carrying their personal lives around in the form of a smartphone.

When my mother was a young adult in her first job, there was no such thing as communicating with people other than your clients or coworkers while performing your job. You simply couldn't shoot a friend a message in the middle of the work day. If you wanted to make dinner plans with your spouse, you did it at home and before you stepped into the office.

Today, it is not only possible to contact friends while at work, but the ways in which you can do it are constantly expanding. With the proliferation and popularity of social networks like Twitter, Facebook, and Instagram, it can be hard to abstain from checking up on your personal life while at work.

Social media continues to become more ingrained in our society. However, Boomers do not even recognize the need to use social media to connect with their personal lives while at work. This type of relationship with technology simply doesn't exist for them.

Remember when I had you picture yourself as a Baby Boomer in 1968?

If you *are* a Boomer, this wasn't hard to do. If you're a member of a younger generation, you might have been surprised to realize how strict the divide between work and life used to be. Because of this, it's not hard to understand why a Boomer wouldn't recognize the need for social media while at work.

After all, Boomers are hard-wired to turn off their personal lives as soon as they enter the workplace. Therefore, using a digital network to stay in touch with family and friends isn't a natural response for them, at least not during the work day.

While Boomers are definitely adapting to the freedoms of technology inside the workplace, they do not utilize new technology in the same way other, younger generations might. This is not for lack of knowledge or an unwillingness to try new things. Baby Boomers do not and have never truly needed access to technology such as social media in order to stay connected at work. They are primed for performing their job without access to this technology because they have lived and worked without it for years.

When asked how unplugging from email, text, and social media during work hours would affect their life, one Boomer's response was, "Being unplugged during the work day would otherwise not really have an impact on my life, once I got used to it. I don't take my phone to meetings so it wouldn't be a big deal."

Email and texting for personal reasons at work can affect a Boomer's job satisfaction. Social media, on the other hand, is not necessary at all for a Boomer to be satisfied at work or with his life in general.

When asked how they would feel if they had to unplug at work, one Boomer replies, "This is completely understandable and I would have no issue doing so. However, I need access to the web and my work email in order to do my job efficiently."

Using technology to get work done is a no-brainer. However, using technology at work in order to stay connected with family and friends is not as necessary for someone of the Boomer generation. As long as tools like texting and email are available, a Boomer isn't likely to feel that their autonomy is stifled at work.

Baby Boomers can function without technology that connects them to their personal lives because they don't need to be connected all the time in a 24/7 fashion.

Millennials, on the other hand, are a different story.

Part IV

Millennials

7

Technology Use For Work: Leveraging Digital Tools

My son figured out how a computer mouse works when he was two years old. I remember sitting with him, showing him how to play a children's computer game.

The object of the game was to move the mouse over an image, such as a teddy bear, in order to make the bear dance. Before I could spend much time showing him how this worked, the phone rang. I was barely on the call for five minutes when I turned back and realized he had already mastered the game.

From that point on, a connection existed in his brain. He understood that moving the physical mouse would cause the cursor on the screen to move in response.

For an adult, this might be a simple step toward learning how to work a computer. For my toddler, this was the beginning of his relationship with digital technology, the start of a learning curve that, for him, would make navigating digital systems as natural as navigating the physical world.

My kids weren't introduced to technology, you see. They were born into it.

From computer games to Nintendo Game Boy, my kids have been interacting with tech since before they had cell phones. They are hard-wired to not only understand technology, but to embrace it. Technology in all its forms has become an ingrained part of their lives and this translates directly into the workplace.

People like to say that Millennials are lazy. Self-absorbed. Entitled.

I find these labels appalling no matter the generation they might be assigned to.

Millennials are different. They approach work and life differently than any generation before them and this is not a bad thing.

When your passion is blending human systems, you begin to see that different does not equal wrong. If we all adopt this mantra we could learn a lot from one another.

Millennials exemplify the concept of work-life fusion. They live and practice it on a daily basis, perhaps unaware that there is any other way to manage their work and personal lives.

The Millennials aren't children any longer. At 75 million and growing, they are the largest generation to date and are quickly becoming major players in the workforce. Due to their early immersion in technology, having access to tools like email, texting, and social media can have an impact on them at work.

Most notably, Millennials use technology to stay connected to their personal lives during the day. However, there are also ways that Millennials use technology to get work done.

Email, for instance, is an important aspect of a Millennial's work life. Using email to get work done gives Millennials a greater sense of autonomy in their jobs.

A Millennial, like my son, needs access to email because it makes him feel that his job permits him to decide how to go about doing his work. This kind of technological freedom in the workplace is greatly valued by Millennials.

A tool that can make Millennials more satisfied with their jobs is the ability to text to get work done. Using text or instant messaging to accomplish work tasks reflects positively upon how much satisfaction and enjoyment a Millennial derives from his job.

When it comes to social media, Millennials don't require it to get work done. Similar to Boomers, Millennials don't feel that they need access to social networking sites for accomplishing work tasks. A Millennial would still consider herself to have freedom and independence in her job if social media wasn't available at work.

This might be because social media is a relatively recent phenomenon. Both email and texting are technologies that have been around for over twenty years. Sites like Facebook and Twitter, on the other hand, didn't exist until the early 2000's.

Another explanation is that it depends on the type of work you do, whether you need access to social media for work. For example, a social media marketer would most definitely require social media in order to complete her work, whereas a typical administrative assistant might not.

All in all, email is the most essential tool for Millennials when it comes to getting work done. Access to email can affect Millennial job satisfaction, their work-life satisfaction, and also their satisfaction with life in general.

Millennials consider texting and instant messaging in the workplace to be additional conveniences, but these tools can also make them happier with their jobs.

Social media, on the other hand, is not as necessary for performing work duties. Where social media plays the largest role is in staying connected to one's personal life while at work. Millennials feel this in a way that most Baby Boomers do not.

8

Technology Use For Personal Life: The Virtual State of Mind

For Millennials, having access to technology in order to stay connected with family and friends is crucial.

Even in the workplace, Millennials are always on. They've been conditioned from birth to use technology to communicate wherever and whenever.

When my daughter was thirteen, she started carrying a cell phone. The technology had been around for a while, but she didn't really need a phone until the end of middle school. Not long after, both my sons wanted phones as well—and not just the trendy flip phone. They needed the newest model, complete with a foldout keyboard that made texting so much easier.

For my kids, this was the main objective of having a cell phone. Whereas I wanted my daughter to have a phone so she could call me in case of emergencies, she wanted it so she could text her friends. In this way, Millennials became the first generation of texters, adopting this new technology faster than anyone else.

This eager and fervent embrace of technology greatly defines the Millennial generation.

Today, Americans text more than they place phone calls. Texting surpassed calls almost a decade ago as the sending of brief messages became easier than calling someone up and hoping you didn't get their voice mail, or worse, the dreaded call waiting tone.[10]

Not only do Millennials text more than they call people, they're more likely to text friends and family than they are to use email to stay in touch.

At work, Millennials use email to stay connected to their personal lives. Email, in this case, is more of a convenience than a necessity. Having access to personal email at work helps a Millennial feel satisfied with the conditions of her life in general, but it doesn't affect how much a Millennial likes her job.

Texting in the workplace is quite different. Since texting is an important way that Millennials stay connected to their lives, even while at work, the availability of texting, or lack thereof, can have an enormous impact. The personal freedom associated with the ability to text at work in order to remain connected to personal life impacts all manner of satisfaction for Millennials.

Texting, therefore, is a powerful tool in the lives of Millennials. If a Millennial cannot text at work for personal life management, he will be less satisfied with his job and dissatisfied with the way he is dividing his time between personal and work responsibilities. In addition, a Millennial without access to texting will be less happy with life.

As you might recall, Boomers are in strong agreement with Millennials here. Members of both the Baby Boomer and Millennial generations need to be able to text while at work in order to stay in contact with friends and family. If they cannot, they will be largely dissatisfied.

But for Millennials, texting isn't the only tool that has this kind of power.

Facebook, Twitter, LinkedIn, YouTube.

These have become household names, but not so long ago no one had even heard of the term 'social media'.

In the early 2000's, people wrote, read, and commented on blogs if they wanted to socialize on "the net". It wasn't until sites like MySpace and LinkedIn first rose to prominence that the essence of social media was born. Today, Facebook boasts over a billion users.[11]

The drivers of this social media craze are no doubt Millennials. While people young and old are participating, Millennials have a special bond with this technology. Some have grown up on virtual social networks, especially Facebook and Twitter, and their personal lives are deeply entwined with these sites.

Because of this, social media usage in order to stay connected at work is critical for Millennials. Being able to use social media while at work directly impacts all levels of satisfaction as well as their sense of job freedom and autonomy.

This means that if social media is restricted in the workplace, a Millennial will likely be less satisfied with her job as well as unhappy with the way she is dividing her time between work and personal life. Millennials who can't use social media at work also feel less content with their life in general. These well-being issues have strong implications for employers.

Millennials rate the highest when it comes to a need for digital connectivity while at work. They also require the strongest connection to personal life while at work.

In this way, technology is non-negotiable for Millennials in the workplace. They haven't simply adapted to new technology, they've been immersed in it for most of their lives and it's because of this immersion that Millennials are the first truly fused generation. For them, there is no strict divide between work and life. Utilizing technology, they are able to manage their work and life responsibilities concurrently rather than individually.

The way Millennials use and view technology differs greatly from the generations before them. Growing up with digital tools has given them a different perspective when it comes to managing one's job and personal life. This relationship with technology has led to the new model of work-life fusion.

While Boomers do not necessarily need certain technology at work, Millennials consider this technology essential for satisfaction and well-being.

To illustrate this mentality, I asked some Millennial college students how they would feel if their boss told them to unplug from email, text, and social media during work hours.

A natural Millennial response was, "I would feel extremely disconnected".

Another student said she would feel unsettled because checking email, and even text, is a force of habit. Not being able to do so would be a big adjustment.

Overall, texting and social media are essential for a Millennial at work when it comes to staying connected to personal life. Without the ability to text or check social media, a Millennial will be dissatisfied with his job and extremely stressed.

Not being able to access technology goes against the way Millennials have operated since childhood. Technology has become very much a part of the Millennial and the prime way one navigates her work and personal life. Taking that away is somewhat equivalent to banishing the telephone from a Boomer's early workplace and asking that he do his job regardless.

Without technology such as their smartphones, Millennials feel isolated from friends and family. If a work environment does not accommodate their needs, they have no issue with leaving the job.

As one Millennial puts it, being forced to refrain from email, text, and social media makes him feel "frustrated and unplugged".

When asked if this would change how satisfied they are with their job, Millennials say that they would be less satisfied, especially if the rule was strictly enforced.

"It would make me less satisfied because I would feel more restricted and that there was a lack of trust."

Additionally, Millennials are less happy with their lives when they have to work a job in which they aren't allowed to use technology to stay connected to family and friends. The reasoning for this is perhaps the fact that technology is so prevalent. Limiting certain tools is effectively saying that Millennials can't be trusted to get their work done.

In the words of one student, "I believe technology should be a choice and if it is affecting my productivity, I should be the one to stop it".

There is no proof that Millennials aren't as productive or diligent as the generations preceding them. Although labeled as lazy, Millennials simply do things differently. They manage their work and personal lives simultaneously, in a way that Baby Boomers never had an opportunity to experience.

Although Millennials are always connected to their personal lives at work, the same is true in reverse. When they are not at work, Millennials continue to tend to work issues in their personal domains, sometimes working far outside of traditional hours.

Just as Millennials are only a text or email away from their personal lives, so it is with their employers. For them, location and time are irrelevant. In a fused world, everything happens all the time and everything should be tended to as such.

Whether they work for themselves or for a company, a Millennial's schedule varies drastically when compared to a Boomer twenty years ago. The term "9 to 5" job has become a misnomer in a world of same-day delivery and 24/7 availability. Millennials are always connected and therefore can always be reached.

As new possibilities like working from home are established, work-life fusion only continues to spread and evolve. It has become evident that policies related to technology at work, do and will continue to impact worker well-being.

In summary, Millennials require access to texting and social media while at work in order to tend to personal responsibilities. These technologies are critical because they can affect a Millennial's sense of freedom and autonomy. When their autonomy is stifled, Millennials are less satisfied with their jobs and as a result, will look elsewhere.

Part V

Future

9

The Stress Factor

People of all ages enjoy more satisfaction with their lives if they can plug in at work.

While people of different ages do not use the same tools at work, they all agree on one. To stay connected to life while at work, texting is the tool of choice. Whether or not this tool's availability affects their job autonomy, they all agree that being able to text changes how satisfied they feel with their lives.

Beyond this common ground, each generation uses different tools for work and life management. Boomers prefer tools like email and texting which heightens their job satisfaction and gives them a greater sense of freedom and autonomy at work.

Not surprisingly, Millennials use and require the most technology while at work. As the first truly fused generation, they tend to both work tasks and personal life simultaneously. This kind of fused approach requires tools like texting and social media in order for them to remain connected with both aspects of their lives and blend them together accordingly. Without being able to use such tools, a Millennial's satisfaction at work suffers in a number of ways. Not only this, but their satisfaction with life suffers as well.

The tools you use and how they affect your sense of job autonomy is different depending on your age. If your context is work-life fusion and this is how you function, then tools that connect you to friends and family while at work will aid in your sense of freedom and autonomy. This has been reported to reduce stress, which ultimately leads to increased job satisfaction.

What's interesting about Millennials is that, except using email to get work done, the tools leveraged by them are all in an effort to stay connected to personal life. Texting and social media are both used to stay connected to life outside of work. There is a strong connection between these tools and a Millennial's sense of freedom and autonomy in her job.

It is clear that people of all ages are using the technology available today. Access to such technology can improve satisfaction levels, whether they're related to one's job or one's personal life. At the same time, however, the more technological immersion a person has experienced in their lifetime, the more stressed they feel at work if they can't use technology to remain connected to friends and family.

This is the key difference between Boomers and Millennials. While Boomers utilize and derive satisfaction from technology, they are able to work without some tools if necessary. They do not experience as much stress as Millennials when asked to disconnect from their phones and other technology.

People of the Baby Boomer generation appreciate new technology, but are able to revert back to the mentality of shutting off their personal lives while at work. On the contrary, Millennials cannot do this without experiencing discomfort and some form of stress while attempting to do their jobs.

Boomers are mostly unaffected by work restrictions about when and how they can use technology to connect to their personal lives.

In one survey, I asked Boomers whether being unplugged at work, especially from email, text, and social media, would make them feel stressed or not. Many people of this generation responded that they definitely would not be stressed.

As one Boomer explains, "I like access to email and the Internet but I am not constantly on social media, texting people, etc. so this would not be a catastrophe."

When asked the same question, Millennials reported that they would be more stressed at work without access to these tools. When asked why they would be stressed, a common response was that they would feel as if they were out of the loop and missing out on important interactions. As one Millennial puts it, "Work isn't all my life".

The stress factor is the most important difference between Baby Boomers and Millennials. While Boomers have no issue dissociating from certain technologies while at work, many Millennials do.

The younger you are, the more wired you are to use and rely on technology. This is the result of immersion in technology from an early age and our continued shift into digital environments.

The dawn of the digital age has brought about rapid change in all areas of our lives, especially how we live and work. These changes affect everyone, including the overlooked "middle-child", Generation X.

10

Generation X: The Sandwich Generation

For comparison purposes, I've focused primarily on explaining the needs of Baby Boomers and Millennials in the workplace. This is due to the greater age gap and therefore larger difference in the way each approaches and experiences technology at work. However, I would be remiss not to mention my generation.

In the workplace, Gen Xers like technology and agree that using email to get work done is an important aspect of work life. Like Millennials, this tool gives us a greater sense of autonomy in our jobs.

At work, Gen Xers are content with life as long as we can text family and our personal network and beyond that, we simply adapt and go along our merry way. This is most likely a result of our upbringing as well as our relation to neighboring generations.

As a member of Gen X, I grew up in a time of relative peace and prosperity. My mom worked as a legal secretary during the day while my father worked as a police officer. I would return from school each day with no one but my parakeet to greet me.

At six years old, I'd let myself in with the key that had been safety-pinned to my undershirt. I'd get a snack, do my homework and then play with my dolls until my mom came home.

I wasn't aware of it at the time, but I learned independence and self-sufficiency at an early age. This was typical for a Gen X kid, born at a time when mothers were going to work and before the daycare system was developed.

Sometimes known as "latch key" kids, Generation X is also called the sandwich generation. This is partly because Gen X is effectively sandwiched between two much larger generations, the Baby Boomers and Millennials.

Due to their smaller size, Gen X faces unique problems in the workplace. With Boomers staying in the workforce longer, holding upper level jobs, and Millennials entering to take lower level jobs, it is easy for Gen Xers to be squeezed out. If nothing else, they face an unprecedented level of competition for jobs from two different directions in the hierarchy.

For example, it was customary in the past for people to be promoted based on age and time spent working for the company. It was unusual for a young worker to have older people reporting to them. Today, however, this is a normal occurrence.

This sandwiched phenomenon does not just happen at work. Because of where we landed on the time continuum, my generation is responsible for supporting both aging parents and growing children simultaneously.

At the same time, if you look closely at the market system, marketers haven't done extensive research or spent much money targeting Gen X and their preferences when it comes to clothing, food, and other products.

We have been largely overlooked when it comes to marketing. This is because it's been far more lucrative to cater to the tastes of the Boomers and Millennials, each about 75 million strong. Why waste production and operation dollars on the mere 65 million when tapping the larger markets would prove more fruitful?

As a Gen Xer, I can tell you that I've had to decide which clothing trend fits my lifestyle better, the Boomers' or the Millennials'. Companies won't spend millions designing products to attract Gen X when the same investment could serve to attract a larger number of a different group.

Think of it this way: Suppose you're selling a $10 product. Would you rather capture sales from 10% of 75 million or 10% of 65 million? The difference in profit is $10 million! It's a no-brainer for businesses and it's why for years I have browsed countless shelves and racks, uninterested in the popular products.

Because of this and other issues that confirm the sandwiched nature of Gen Xers, we have become a casual and open group. Gen Xers have spent their lives adapting to the tastes and customs of both Boomers and Millennials and, as a result, have become a versatile breed.

Like Millennials, they adopt new technology and like Boomers, they don't necessarily need technology at work. However, access to texting and other tools is certainly a plus.

Gen Xers manage their work and personal lives concurrently when it suits them. In this way, work and life no longer exist as separate domains in need of a precarious balancing act. With technology, work and life can now exist together, in a fused state in which they are one.

You've no doubt experienced it yourself:

The phone call from a partner or spouse that you think nothing of answering at work.

The work email you think nothing of replying to while at home enjoying your free time.

Maybe you work at home and have already obliterated the physical environment of the "workplace".

If you were born after the Boomer generation, you are probably living your life in the context of work-life fusion. You do not balance and you do not compartmentalize. Work and personal life happen simultaneously and all the time.

Boomers are hard-wired for the separation of work and life. As such, they will always default to this when necessary since they grew up without immersion in digital technology. Even with tools like social media available, it is their normal to turn their personal lives off when they need to focus on work.

In a nutshell, Gen Xers require the use of email in order to accomplish work tasks. Without this technology, they would be very unhappy indeed.

On the other hand, tools like texting and social media aren't as necessary. Gen Xers experience more life satisfaction if they can text their family and friends while at work, but this is the extent of their technological needs when it comes to work-life management.

In short, Gen Xers are embracing technology and work-life fusion, but can be happy at work without it. This is in stark contrast to Millennials who are actually stressed and unhappy if they find themselves in a work culture that does not support work-life fusion.

With different attitudes like these mixing in the workplace, generational sensitivity becomes a primary concern. The nature of our work environment only continues to change, from a generational standpoint as well as a technological one.

11

Fusion: The New Normal

By the year 2020, Millennials will make up 50% of the global workforce.[12] The support of a technological environment at work is a requirement for this generation because Millennials are psychologically impacted by the availability of digital tools at work. If they can't access these tools, they feel a loss of freedom and autonomy in their jobs which can bode badly for employers wishing to retain Millennial talent.

Certain technologies at work can make people feel in control of their jobs, leading to greater job and work-life satisfaction. In other words, if people work in an environment that supports technology, they feel they have personal autonomy in getting their jobs done. This reduces their stress and may cause them to feel that their employer trusts them.

When technology is supported at work, everyone experiences positive feelings of satisfaction with their lives because they are able to satisfy their need to administer to social obligations while at work. For Millennials, in particular, this is imperative. Quality of work life issues abound with the reality of their need to remain connected to family and personal life while at work.

When smartphones first started to gain in popularity, there was a question in some workplaces as to whether or not it was appropriate for employees to be using their phones for personal reasons during work hours.

As Millennials become the majority in the workforce and as work-life fusion becomes the new norm, these apprehensions are likely to disappear. Although it varies depending on your type of work, technology only continues to infiltrate our work environments and our lives.

Understanding work-life fusion and how Millennials function in the workplace is crucial for companies and businesses wishing to retain employees. Clearly, it is important that people remain satisfied with their jobs. In the future, employers who can support the needs of their Millennial employees will be able to effectively reduce turnover and become more profitable.

As we've seen, when Millennials feel restricted and confined, they are less satisfied with their jobs and therefore more likely to leave them. Perhaps because of this, many Millennial workers have been labeled as "job hoppers".

Unlike generations before them, Millennials are not of the mindset that they will have the same employer for life. In fact, very rarely does this occur anymore. Millennials, and even younger generations, are opting for freedom and quality of life over monetary gain or status.

According to the Bureau of Labor Statistics, a person born in the latter years of the Baby Boom had an average of 11 jobs between the ages of 18 to 48.[13] Millennials are expected to have far more, staying in some jobs for two years or less.

Not only this, but Millennials are looking for something that is more than just a job. They seek a steady income and autonomous work environment, but also a career that compliments their lifestyle and makes them happier and more satisfied with their lives.

Millennials are more likely to quit traditional jobs to pursue passion projects, seek jobs geared toward the social good, and value creativity and entrepreneurship.[14]

In this context, work-life fusion is on the rise: the search not only for work that can support a life, but work that compliments life. Not just work that pays the bills, but work that represents who you are as a person. When you combine work and life to the point that they are fluid, this search for satisfying and meaningful work is the natural result.

There is no question that the Millennial generation is leading organizations to rethink how they structure and manage their work environments. The nature of work is changing for good and as time progresses, even the term "workplace" becomes a less concrete concept.

Children continue to be exposed to the Internet, technology, and all that comes with it at younger and younger ages. Millennials didn't have social media from the time of their birth, but the majority of Generation Z will. As future generations are born and technology continues to advance, work-life fusion will redefine the ways in which we live and work.

For the time being, Boomers, Gen Xers, and Millennials must share the workplace. As each generation approaches work-life management differently, so does each person have a different experience with technology. Although technology comes with its caveats, it can change our lives for the better. As long as we seek first to understand, we can continue to foster cross-generational relationships; and the stronger our relationships, the more effectively we can work together as work-life fusion becomes our new normal.

FUSION CHECK

Do you remember which tools impact a person's sense of freedom and autonomy at work?

Don't worry, we made a list for you:

BOOMERS

——Getting Work Done——

Tools for Freedom:
Text/IM

Tools for Convenience:
Email
Social Media

Employer Implications:

- Make text and instant messaging services readily available for work related communications

- Keep supporting email environments

——Personal Life——

Tools for Freedom:
Text/IM
Email

Tools for Convenience:
No additional tools needed

Employer Implications:

- Allow texting for personal purposes while at work

- Allow access to personal email in the workplace

MILLENNIALS

——Getting Work Done——

Tools for Freedom:
Email

Tools for Convenience:
Text/IM

Employer Implications:

- Make email services readily available for organizational communication

- Consider a culture that supports texting/IM use for work when the need arises

——Personal Life——

Tools for Freedom:
Text/IM
Social Media

Tools for Convenience:
Email

Employer Implications:

- Allow access to smartphones while at work for both texting and social media

- Be mindful of the personal connection Millennials require to feel happy and secure at work. They will work harder for you 24/7 if they can be fused 24/7.

GEN X

——Getting Work Done——

Tools for Freedom:
Email

Tools for Convenience:
No additional tools needed

Employer Implications:

- Make email services readily available for organizational communication

——Personal Life——

Tools for Freedom:
None—we'll use whatever's available

Tools for Convenience:
Text/IM

Employer Implications:

- Allow texting at work for personal life management

Acknowledgments

I would like to thank my daughter, Eilysh, for her amazing skill and patience in making this book a reality. I have always known her to be a talented writer, but her penchant for project management kept me on task. Without her incredible intellect and ability, sharing what I've discovered with an audience beyond the research world would have been impossible. It is thanks to her technical savviness that we can offer this information in both an e-book and print format.

A big thank you also goes to our editor, Evelyn P. Raimondo Kaiser, Esq. (mother and grandmother of the authors) for taking time out of her busy schedule to review our manuscript. You completed our generational trifecta. Now, a Boomer, Gen Xer, and Millennial have all had a hand in making this book what it is.

Thank you to our beta readers: Monish Pahilajani, Katie Tretter, and Brittany Leoboldt, whose suggestions and feedback were invaluable and helped make this book a better reading experience for all.

Huge thanks to Leigh Haeger for designing the awesome spiral graphic that appears on the cover. We are grateful for the time you spent bringing our cover ideas to life.

Special thanks to everyone who advised us, answered questions and shared perspectives on using technology and tools at work. Your insights and support made this book richer.

I would be remiss in not thanking Laurie A. Branch, Ph.D. and Tony Lingham, Ph.D. for support and advisement during the two studies leading up to the one this book is based on. You are friends for life. We rely on each other!

About the Authors

Donna L. Haeger, Ph.D.

Donna is a member of Generation X and a Professor of Business Education at <u>Cornell University</u>. She is dedicated to cultivating business synergy by blending human and analytical systems. Her research interests are in the area of technology in the workplace, leadership and organizational behavior with a focus on influence and intergenerational exchanges. Publishing this book has been a career-long goal.

When she's not working, Donna has an insatiable desire to travel and see new places. She enjoys time with her family and friends, especially if it is spent on a beach.

Eilysh Haeger

Eily is a Millennial writer passionate about storytelling and the power of the written word. This is her first book. She's set herself a goal to continue publishing fiction and non-fiction.

She is also interested in instructional design and creating great, informative content.

When Eily's not busy writing or planning her next project, you can find her reading, baking brownies, or playing with her cats. To find out what Eily's up to, follow her writing journey at:

writervice.wordpress.com

If you enjoyed this book and found it to be informative, please leave a review on Amazon.

Thank you!

References

[1] Fry, R. (2015, May 11). Millennials surpass Gen Xers as the largest generation in U.S. labor force.

[2] Kossek, E. E., Lautsch, B. A., & Easton, S. C. (2005). Telecommuting, control, and boundary management: Correlates of policy use and practice, job control, and work-family effectiveness. *Journal of Vocational Behaviors, 68*, 347-367.

[3] Proserio, L., & Gioia, D. (2007). Teaching the Virtual Generation. *Academy of Management Journal*, 69-80.

[4] Haeger, D., & Lingham, T. (2013). Intergenerational Collisions and Leadership in the 21st Century. Journal of Intergenerational Relationships.11:286-303.

[5] Haeger, D., & Lingham, T. (2014). A Trend Toward Work-Life Fusion: A Multi-Generational Shift in Technology Use at Work. Technological Forecasting and Social Change. 89:316-325.

[6] Haeger, D. (2017), Work-Life Fusion: Scale Refinement, Validation, and Multi-Generational Analysis: Investigating the extent to which people leverage technological tools to manage work and life issues while at work.

Multivariate analysis confirms impacts on Psychological Job Control, Job Satisfaction, Work Life Satisfaction and Satisfaction with Life.

[7] Partridge, C. (2008). The Technical Development of Internet Email. *IEEE Annals of the History of Computing, 30*(2).

[8] Radicati, S. (Ed.). (2014, April). Email Statistics Report 2014-2018 (Rep.).

[9] Text messaging. (2017, April 18).

[10] In U.S., SMS Text Messaging Tops Mobile Phone Calling. (2008, September 22).

[11] Hale, B. (2016, June 16). The History of Social Media: Social Networking Evolution!

[12] Millennials at work: Reshaping the workplace (Rep.). (2011).

[13] United States of America, U.S. Department of Labor, Bureau of Labor Statistics. (2015, March 31). Number of Jobs Held, Labor Market Activity, and Earnings Growth Among the Youngest Baby Boomers: Results from a Longitudinal Survey.

[14] Ricketts, W. (2014, March 27). Inaugural Creative Jobs Report Reveals New American Dream.

Further Resources

Fry, R. (2016, April 25). Millennials overtake Baby Boomers as America's largest generation.

Research by Donna L. Haeger is available on Google Scholar.

www.ingramcontent.com/pod-product-compliance
Lightning Source LLC
Chambersburg PA
CBHW051344170526
45166CB00002B/950

* 9 7 8 1 5 2 1 1 8 8 5 4 5 *